Let's Try Cartomancy

Divination with Playing Cards:

A Taster Guide for Beginners

Ann J. Clark

First edition published in the UK July 2018

Published by Calico Cat Press

Table of Contents

Introduction

Before the tarot boom took off, playing cards were the most popular card divination method used by fortune-tellers; and while history shows that many different kinds of decks were used in many different kinds of ways, the standard 52 card deck is still used by modern readers to provide valuable insight into the past, present and future.

If you're curious about the art of playing card divination, all you need is a deck of normal playing cards and the information in this taster guide. We have included a variety of examples in the Spreads sections, ranging from simple yes/no readings to full tarot style spreads that allow you to unravel knotty problems or forecast the week or year ahead. You will find a selection of the most common card meanings in the Interpretations chapter, as well as tips to combine cards and interpret patterns to find deeper nuance and spark your intuition.

The basic skills provided should give you a useful foundation if you want to progress in your divination studies or simply amaze your friends and family with your uncanny fortune-telling ability!

Ann J. Clark

Brief History

There are many different theories about the origin of playing cards and their use in divination.

The earliest appearances of playing cards can be seen in China and India in the 900's AD. Indian cards of the time are said to show Hindu gods holding sceptres, swords, cups and rings, while evidence suggests that the Emperor Mu-Tsung played domino cards, a game resembling playing cards, with his wife on the eve of the Chinese New Year 969AD. [1]

Moving on to the 1300 and 1400's, playing cards were found across Europe - one theory places the origin of European cards in a region of Egypt with a Mameluke deck dating from 1400 and comprising of 52 cards with 4 suits – swords, polo sticks, cups and coins. [1]

In Switzerland in 1377, a Basle monk called John of Rheinfelden wrote what is considered the first detailed description of use of a deck of 52 playing cards and Marco Polo is also thought to have brought cards back from his 13th century expeditions to China. There is a theory that the Crusaders carried cards back from their conquests, but the most popular theory is that the cards were brought through India and Egypt by bands of travellers. [1]

Playing cards were used at the French court in 1390 where the mistress of King Charles VI, Odette, had a pack brought by travellers and decorated with Eastern potentates. She then designed her own pack picturing members of the French court – providing the origin of the court cards on the modern deck. It is rumoured that a visiting traveller used the cards to foretell for Odette and the King, and divined the King's secrets. It is also rumoured that Napoleon planned several battles and courted Empress Josephine with playing card divination. [1]

From this came the current standard playing card deck – also originating in France, and thought to have been introduced around the late 15th century, painted by hand or printed with woodblocks. It wasn't until 1832 that playing cards were mass manufactured and while these earlier versions were designed to be viewed from one way up only, the late 19th century saw the introduction of the double headed design we use today.

How Does It Work?

Before You Read

The benefit of using playing cards for divination is you can get them anywhere, they're small enough to carry in a pocket, most homes have at least one deck somewhere, and if not, they're easy to find and inexpensive to buy. Once you've acquired a deck for divination purposes, don't be tempted to use it for playing regular card games – keep your deck in a separate drawer or a special box or pouch, or wrap it in black silk or other material.

Find Your Spread

Before you shuffle and deal your cards, you will need to pick a reading layout to use – this will tell you how many cards you need to deal and help to give context to the reading as the card's position in the spread indicates what point in time and/or aspect of the questioner's life the card refers to.

There are a wide variety of spreads that can be used with a deck of playing cards – the easiest and most popular spreads use the full deck of 52 cards but if you feel up to a challenge, you could try the spreads that use only 32 of the cards.

Interpretations for some cards change when using the 32 card method which is why you will find the information on 32 card spreads in the **Advanced Spreads** section.

Have a look at the basic spreads included in the Spreads section then when you've chosen one for your reading, it's time to shuffle and deal your cards.

Shuffling

While tarot cards must be handled careful during a shuffle, playing cards were designed to be hardier, so use whichever kind of shuffle you prefer. You or the person you're reading for can shuffle for as long as feels comfortable, always keeping your desired question or general issues in mind. Then, keeping the cards face down, cut the cards into multiple piles and reassemble them into one neat stack. How many times the deck is cut and how it's reassembled is purely personal preference – many readers choose to split the deck into 3 piles and reassemble in whatever order feels appropriate at the time, but if you want to do more or less, it's up to you.

Dealing

Another difference between tarot card reading and playing card reading is, most of the time, there's only one way up to read a card so it doesn't matter which way you pick up a card or whether you use a neat deal or a messy deal.

A neat deal is similar to how you would deal cards in a card game. Take the cut and reassembled pack and deal the cards face up in the layout you've chosen.

A messy deal means muddling or sliding the face down cards on the surface of your table to really jumble them up. Once you're satisfied you've messed the cards up enough, pick the cards you feel most drawn to and deal them face up in the layout you've chosen.

Interpreting the Cards

Whether you're reading from a 52 card deck or the modified 32 card deck, the sections that follow will give you suggested keywords to interpret the individual cards and the patterns of multiple cards. The more you use your cards, the easier it will be to remember what each symbolises as the images and meanings will get wired into your brain, and you'll the find it easier to adapt your interpretations.

Before you start to interpret the individual cards, take a look at the bigger picture – is one suit more dominant? Are there more court cards? Are there multiples of one number? This will allow you to get an overview of trends and may alter your interpretation of individual cards.

Now you're ready to interpret the cards individually - take a look at the card and note its position in the spread for context, then look at the interpretations provided in the relevant **Interpretation Keywords** section. As playing cards were originally designed to be read one way up, there are no reversed readings. You will find both negative and positive interpretations for most cards, so if some of the meanings don't feel right then let your intuition guide you to what to leave out and remember that some cards can be changed by their surrounding cards.

Layouts for 52 Cards

All the spreads in this section use the standard 52 card deck, so once you're comfortable with the basics, feel free to have fun and experiment with the more complicated ones or make up a spread of your own!

Yes/No Wish Reading

Good for: a simple reading to learn whether your question or wish will have a positive or negative outcome.

How to do it: While this spread technically uses all 52 cards, you only need to be aware of two - the Nine of Hearts 'wish' card to indicate a positive outcome, and the Ten of Spades 'disappointment' card to indicate the negative outcome.

Shuffle the deck while thinking strongly of your desired wish. Cut the deck and deal face upwards until either the Yes-Wish card or the No-Disappointment card appears. Whichever turns up first is the answer. Easy!

Yes   No

Simple Three Card Spread

Good for: a quick general overview of the questioner's past, present and future.

How to do it: draw three cards and lay them in the row.

The first card indicates past events, the second card indicates the present situation, and the third card indicates how things are likely to turn out in the future.

The Three Wishes Spread

Good for: divining the result of three wishes.

How to do it: shuffle the pack while thinking of three wishes, think of them in order of preference.

The reader cuts the pack, then deals 3 rows of 3 cards. The first row is the first wish, the second row the second wish, the third row the third wish.

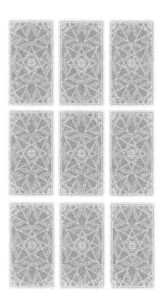

If a row has three court cards it will not come true.

If a row has an ace in it, it will come true.

If none of the above applies, add up the numbers on the cards in a row (using King =13, Queen=12, Jack=11). The lower the value of the cards, the more likely the wish will come true.

Seven Day Spread

Good for: indicating events in the week ahead.

How to do it: draw seven cards and lay them out in a row – you can use a straight row or shape it up in an arch.

The first card shows you the main experiences for the first day in your week, the second card indicates the experiences for the second day, all the way to the end of the week. It's up to you which day of the week you start with.

The Calendar Spread

Good for: showing the likely trends for the year ahead.

How to do it: draw twelve cards and lay them like a clock face. If you wish, you can also draw a card to signify the questioner and put it in the middle to use as a focus. This can either be the joker card, or one of the remaining court cards.

Each card on the clock face represents a month of the year – you can start with January at the top or use whatever the current month is, then work your way around each month in turn.

Standard tarot spreads can also be adapted for reading with playing cards –

Seven Card Horseshoe Spread

Good for: divining the answer to a question, with a little more detail than the shorter spreads, or just used as a general tarot spread.

How to do it: draw seven cards and arrange them in a horseshoe shape. The position of each card in the horseshoe tells you which area of life the card interpretation refers to:

Seven Card Horseshoe Spread

Card no. 1 – Past situation and influences.

Card no. 2 – Present situation.

Card no. 3 - Hidden influences, what is not obvious.

Card no. 4 - Obstacles and problems.

Card no. 5 – Attitude of others around the questioner.

Card no. 6 – Possible action needed by the questioner.

Card no. 7 – Overall outcome.

Celtic Cross Spread

Good for: building a detailed overview of a current issue, its origins and potential outcomes.

How to do it: draw ten cards and arrange them as the next page. When you interpret each card, take into consideration its position in the layout and you will be able to build the story of the reading.

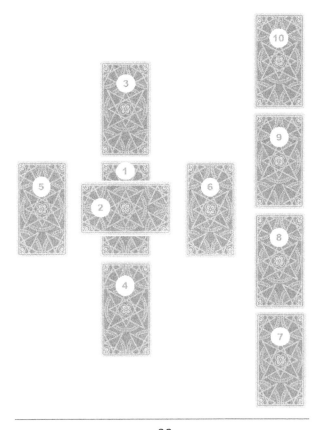

Celtic Cross Spread

Card no. 1 – Present Situation.

Card no. 2 – Crossing card, or current problem.

Card no. 3 – Past Influences.

Card no. 4 – Present Influences.

Card no. 5 – What is on the Surface.

Card no. 6 – What is Hidden.

Card no. 7 – The Questioner's View of the Situation.

Card no. 8 – Views of Others.

Card no. 9 – Hopes & Fears.

Card no. 10 – Outcome.

Interpretation Keywords for 52 Card Readings

Suits - general

If one suit is more represented than the others, then the qualities of that suit can modify the individual cards.

Clubs – ambition, success, career, health, travel, expansion, business partnerships and other business relationships, communication, connections with money, business, and loyalty. Also failure, betrayal and financial worries.

Diamonds – for the life outside the home. Also the suggestion that money and ambitions can only be achieved through hard work. Practical matters, money, property, home, patience, placidity, children, animals.

Hearts – considered lucky, cover emotions and domestic life, love, affection, friendship, marriage, the family. Also ambitions successfully realised. Intuition, relationships, people in their 20's and 30's.

Spades – dangers ahead. Misfortunes, loss, suffering, enemies, treachery, failure. Limitations, challenges, tradition, formal learning, justice, assessment and tradition, older people and ageing.

Court cards vs. numbers

If there are a **majority of court cards**, it suggests that personalities are more important to the questioner than situations.

Four cards of the same value can indicate an extreme version of a result, whether joy or sorrow, good fortune or bad.

Three cards of the same value indicate different forces in harmony.

Two cards of the same value suggest that there is either a conflict of interest, a reconciliation or a new connection, depending on the suits involved.

The **Nine of Hearts** will indicate that a wish will be fulfilled in the area suggested by the most dominant suit surrounding it. (Or will lessen the impact of an overly negative reading)

The **Ten of Spades** will indicate disappointment in the area suggested by the most dominant suit surrounding it. (Or will lessen the impact of an overly positive reading)

Suits – individual cards

 ## Clubs

Associated with the element of fire, the tarot suit of wands.

Ace

Wealth, health, love, happiness, success, peace of mind, happy home life. New beginning in career, new ambition, desire for independence from restricting situation, new channel of communication, new perspective or opportunity for travel, original ideas.

Two

Disappointment, disagreements, opposition. A time to deliberate possible options, need to balance demands of career and health to counter possible exhaustion or stress, take care with a business partnership or work relationship, plans with other people may seem restrictive. Material losses, division between business partners, property or business disputes. Long term plans could meet with delay from another's interference. Watch out for idle chat or malicious gossip.

Three

Marriage bringing money, possibly several marriages, remarriage, declaration of engagement. Communication may involve several people, decisions about travel, opportunity to expand horizons, more energy and input will be needed for increased business or work opportunities/commitments. Events moving slowly, legacies, irritating or unhelpful intervention by others.

Four

Changes for the worse, lies, betrayal. Written communications are better than verbal to clarify intentions. Clear communication and winning the trust of others is essential even if this seems to slow progress. Financial success, prosperity, unexpected but well deserved good luck. Be flexible in your plans.

Five

Advantageous marriage, helpful friends. Make sure you get credit for your input and ideas, rivals may be less than open in their communications, a time to argue and stand your ground in business or work environments. Tiredness and carelessness may cause accidents, care should be taken with health, stress may be caused by over involvement with others. Family divided, disputes about money or property, upsets and unexpected obstacles. Change for the better where partnership is emphasised. Financial rewards from business ventures, good time for marriage plans.

Six

Business success, especially business partnerships. A time for personal creativity and networking to make contacts for the future. Tranquil period at work, time to take a short break from responsibility and recharge. A time where health should improve or remain stable. Run of good luck, great prosperity and material happiness. Established businesses should flourish, new projects will receive financial backing.

Seven

Happiness, prosperity, joy, be careful with prospective partners of the opposite sex as they will cause trouble. Personal success and satisfaction, high levels of creativity and energy, a time to fight for ideals, happiness comes from seeing beyond the immediate returns of a long term goal. Money may be frittered on needless luxuries, foolish speculations or pleasure jaunts. Financial losses and money worries, money wasted. Debts repaid, small gift or money gain. New friendship will bring pleasure. Get legal advice if a contract needs to be signed.

Eight

Reckless chances, disappointment, opposition, a greedy and jealous person who is fond of money. Time of sudden upsurge of energy. Enterprise, changes in career, travel, and lifestyle. Time to act on sudden opportunities. Investments reaping rewards, important documents or letters relating to business or money. Risk of loss by theft or swindle. Time of uncertainty, minor problems could get blown out proportion. Avoid get rich quick schemes.

Nine

Achievements, possibly a new lover, friends being stubborn. Responsibilities may seem overwhelming, burdens should be delegated. Self-doubt and temporary loss of confidence making things worse than they are, press ahead with courage and conviction. Financial matters involving parents, children or lovers. Try not to be obstinate as this could cause friction with others. Possible monetary or other gain due to unforeseen business or marriage proposal.

Ten

Good luck, unexpected money – from a bonus or a win or a legacy or some business idea that takes off quickly. Personal happiness, self-confidence, independence, successful completion of a goal, chance to change direction and learn new skills, an ambition or dream will be realised soon. Stable and comfortable situation, solid and well established prosperity. Material success. Travel could prove profitable or lead to a romantic encounter.

Jack

Dark haired youth, reliable friend who will be of help. Energetic but loses interest if things don't go well, can get absorbed in things to the exclusion of everything else, great communicator but liberal with the truth. Strong interest in money matters but not always reliable or trustworthy. Clever, enterprising, well disposed towards questioner, possibly an admirer or lover.

Queen

Dark haired woman or feminine person, business-like, capable, self-confident, very attractive.

Independent, good organiser and multi tasker, tactful and persuasive and able to get what she wants while keeping others happy. Tendency to overdo things and get exhaustion. Mature, secure, notable for common sense, possibly comfortably off. Warm hearted, charming, quick witted, trustworthy, supportive, wise.

King

Dark haired man or masculine person, honest, generous, helpful, humane, affectionate. Faithful partner who makes others happy. Successful, ambitious, innovator, powerful communicator. Can be insensitive to others needs. Impatient to finish tasks. Idealistic and will not compromise on principles. Good problem solver. Prosperous, secure, reliable. Could also indicate questioner's employer (male or female). Honest and straightforward in dealings. Could be of great assistance.

Diamonds

Associated with the element of earth and the tarot suit pentacles.

Ace

Engagement or wedding ring, letter with good news about money. New financial or practical venture.

Change of home, new home related project, upsurge in prosperity. Erratic good luck. Extraordinary event. New surprises manifesting in existing situations. Energetic or good beginning to course of action. Long awaited letter or important document with welcome news. Financial offer or marriage proposal.

Two

A love affair meets with opposition. Balancing two aspects of life or two areas of responsibility, partnership for a mutually beneficial venture, agreeing a fair division of domestic efforts for equal benefits, an extra source of income. Increase in prosperity but imprudent action should be avoided. Try to relax, look before you leap. Development of love affair or close friendship that may attract others disapproval. Business matters showing progress.

Three

Legal problems, especially if there's a divorce looming. A bad marriage partner who will cause unhappiness. Domestic problems. Also extra commitments or responsibilities that will be long term advantageous, venture with firm foundations, birth or addition to the family. Steady progress with existing problems, good luck through cooperation and help of friends or associates. Litigation possible, partnerships under scrutiny, tact needed to avoid disputes. Cooperation makes better outlooks.

Four

Inheritance or other improvements in finances, changes, troubles. Also limitations in the financial or practical sphere, dilemma about whether to make change or bunker down, difficult decisions or choices at home regarding children, need for patience regarding slow moving property and finance matters. Danger of complacency. Established success, steady good fortune, happiness and prosperity. An old friend may help to reconcile differences. Patience and understanding can resolve matters despite petty squabbles. Careful not to let harsh words or rash actions mar a relationship.

Five

Prosperity, good news, happy family, success in business or other enterprises, children behaving. Build on what has been achieved, plans should be modified not abandoned, find a new source of help or advice, may feel isolated by temporary obstacles. Troubles and conflicts from clash of ideas or profound difference of opinion. Joyful news of a birth or child's achievement. New ventures favoured. Small financial loss offset by exciting business opportunity.

Six

Problems with marriage, especially second marriages. Avoid taking on too many commitments, pay attention to the small print and documents, keep a tight grip on finances, family matters may take up your time, try and find time for reflection and conserving energy. A feeling of happiness that makes any activity seem worthwhile and pleasurable. Marital difficulties, possible separation or divorce though a reconciliation may be possible.

Seven

A gift or surprise, heavy losses. Children or animals may bring joy, trust dreams and intuition as well as common sense. Long term plans are looking good. Domestic and financial matters in harmony. Passionate relationship, strong bonds between partners, physical satisfaction and comfort of any sort. Surprise news will be uplifting. Upsets short lived. Minor problems or disputes at work or home due to petty jealousy, misunderstandings or unkind gossip.

Eight

A marriage late in life which may not be good, journey leading to new relationship, also plans and ideas. New skills are indicated in the money making or practical spheres. Restlessness should be channelled into tangible improvements. Current financial or domestic matters may change suddenly, there may be a house move or refurbishment. Exciting news, messages from afar, adventurous holidays, eventful journeys, change, can indicate study of academic work particularly in the physical sciences. Romance and travel linked especially for very young or elderly. Fortune fluctuations, windfall or small financial loss.

Nine

Restlessness, good surprise regarding money. Better results will be seen from independent thought and action. Put personal interest first, expand horizons and speculate for better chance of success. Birth or marriage, eventful relationship, prosperity, productive disagreements, changes for better. Initiative leads to opportunities for romance, increased income or more enjoyable social life. Business deals, change of residence or occupation all bode well.

Ten

Money, journeys, marriage, changes, possible help from a married man who lives in the country. New permanent domestic commitment or completion of other plans and practical matters, financial success, happiness in home and family. Happy end to turmoil, well-earned holiday, rewards from hard work. Improved finances may help secure the future. Planned journey with unforeseen benefit such as job offer, business expansion opportunity, new romance.

Jack

A fair haired relative who is selfish, not too reliable, dishonest and only interested in their own requirements and opinions. Though, also, practical reliable younger person whose common sense and support will help. Pushy, impulsive, has considerable courage and tenacity. Personable. May bring news, if unwelcome news not disastrous. Guard against dishonesty.

Queen

Fair haired woman or feminine person, flirtatious, sophisticated and fond of socialising. Practical, organised, good at sorting out problems and making people feel at home. Mature, forceful, bossy. May pose a threat to the questioner's love life or interfere with business affairs. Needs careful handling so need to be tactful with them.

King

Fair haired man or masculine person, obstinate, quick tempered, powerful, helpful to the questioner. Sometimes considered dull, but reliable, impatient, shows affection through deeds not words. Extremely energetic, mature, finds it difficult to relax. Ambitious, influential, power to help or hinder. Any propositions from him should be considered carefully.

 ### *Hearts*

Associated with the element of water and the tarot suit of cups.

Ace

Joy, love, friendship, affection, start of a romance, the home. Sudden burst of intuition should be trusted, unrequited love, new start after emotional or romantic set back, unexpected happiness. Domestic happiness. Birth, marriage proposal, new friendship, reunion.

Two

Success, happiness, luck, prosperity, an engagement, possibly a marriage. Reconciliation between two people with opposing views, mending of old quarrels, growing friendship, two elements of life coming together, love match, emotional partnership rather than financial. Consolidation of current partnership or new romantic liaison. Friendships and close personal ties should flourish. Greater fortune than anticipated.

Three

Friends, sociability, enjoyable encounters with others. The questioner may need to be cautious, rash statements will upset others. Stress from emotional pressure or blackmail, rivalry in love or friendship, emotional conflicts with two people seeking sympathy or favour. Difficult choice to be made, try to defer decision until all possibilities can be considered.

Four

A journey or changes, delays, postponements. Another person's commitment may be questionable, emotional choices, feelings of restlessness and emotional dissatisfaction. Solid emotional relationships are indicated, enduring friendships or love. Time of change in employment or residence. Marriage or remarriage a possibility for mature questioners.

Five

Money, indecisiveness, jealous or unreliable people around. Unwise passions, accept the reality of existing relationship and not the idealised version, misunderstandings, need to communicate from the heart. Unsure love, emotional disturbances, love that sours. Put off important decisions or dramatic changes to your life – take a short break, relax and get thoughts in order before tackling issues.

Six

A generous person, a shoulder to cry on, shared confidences, unexpected propositions, unexpected good luck, pleasant invitations, established affection. Reconciliation with older people, accepting different attitudes still allow for love or friendship, positive influence of loyal friends, harmony and quiet contentment in relationships. Happy family news, possibly engagement or child's achievement. Others may try to take advantage of your good nature, avoid taking on too much.

Seven

Unfaithful or unreliable person, news, false hopes, broken promises. Intuition, dreams, telepathic communication, trust your instincts, colleagues or acquaintances will be on the same wavelength and cooperative. Love fulfilled, passionate and happy sexual relationships. Good time for romance, keep plans flexible, friend or colleague could let you down at last moment, anticipated event could be cancelled without warning.

Eight

Invitations, festivities, visits and visitors, journeys for pleasure, meals in good company. Moving to a new phase in relationship. Beware of jealousy. A time to end potentially destructive emotional attachments or emotional blackmail. Love that is intellectual, calm and reasoned. Love letters, phone calls from loved ones, communication about romantic matters. Also indications of books concerning love and human emotions. Journey or outing could lead to romantic encounter which may develop into something enduring.

Nine

Known as the 'Wish' card – dreams will come true. An improvement in circumstances, health, wealth, status, esteem. Emotional independence, self-confidence. Boosts the cards around it. Existing misunderstandings will soon be resolved, success in whatever closest to the questioner's heart (nearest card suits will indicate area).

Ten

Good luck, love, joy, improves any bad cards surrounding it, confirms the benefits of other good cards in the spread. Happy marriages, permanent relationships, emotional happiness and fulfilment through others, satisfaction from caring for others, generosity to others. Solid emotion based on material happiness and financial prosperity. Happiness in love, fulfilling domestic situation, business success. Opportunity to secure the future may arise unexpectedly – do not hesitate to take it.

Jack

A fair haired youth or emotionally vulnerable older person, a good friend, nearby cards will illuminate their intentions. Incurable romantic who seeks perfection in love. May tend towards sentiment over reality. Impulsive affection. Amiable, sincere, possibly long standing friend or relative. Could be instrumental in introducing questioner to someone emotionally important.

Queen

A fair haired woman or feminine person, kindly, loving, who will be good to the questioner, faithful, trustworthy, affectionate. Mature woman possessed of strong emotions. Sentimentalist who could become too overwhelmed by others sorrows and emotional needs that they loses their own identity, may hold people back from their own emotional independence. Warm hearted, mature, has questioner's best interests at heart. Kind, sensible, offers sound advice, practical help, comfort.

King

Fair haired man or masculine person, good natured, impetuous, kind, loving and affectionate and will give good advice. May have trouble handling their own emotions while caring more for others' troubles. Great romantic but easily tempted and flattered, charismatic, makes people feel valued and special. Sociable, generous, enthusiastic, well disposed towards questioner, may lack discretion and not always a wise judge. Also an indication that minor money problems will be short lived.

Spades

Associated with the element of air and the tarot suit of swords.

Ace

Love affairs, passion, obsession, deceitful friends, emotional conflict. New beginning after difficulty or sorrow, new challenge will open doors, new form of learning, sudden recourse to justice. New and exciting adventurers with unknown results. Look to the suits of the cards nearby to see what area the new beginning applies to. Challenge. Underlying tensions or problems are about to erupt which may be distressing but will clear the air long term.

Two

Separation, scandal, gossip, betrayal. Choice between two unattractive options but a choice must be made. Need for logic to solve conflict, need to decide which of two options is true. Moving forward, dynamic development of something. Ideas, hopes or aspirations starting to take form. A hopeful start. Change is coming. New home or new job or end of relationship. Feeling of loss leading to improved circumstances.

Three

Faithlessness, partings, marriage with a wealthy partner who is fickle and unreliable. Malice or rivalry needs to be solved by reason. Time and effort will be needed to overcome challenges or obstacles and reach success. Facts that seem unimportant will come in useful at a later date. Meeting or conference, sharing of ideas, airy ideas being solidified, prudent or careful consideration of future plans needed. Caution and prudence needed in general. Conflict will arise in partnerships if a third party is allowed to interfere.

Four

Jealousy, illness, business or money worries. Past disappointments or betrayals are creating inner fears that cause obstacles and limitations. Injustices need to be set aside or resolved. Losses must be accepted to move on. Solid progress on realising an idea. Foresight will improve chances of good luck and prosperity.   Delayed or disrupted plans, broken promises, support at home lacking. Fresh opportunities on the way.

Five

Anxieties with eventual success, good marriage, domestic happiness, bad tempered people around the questioner but outside the home environment. Try being a little less open about your intentions, be sure of your facts to avoid hidden spite or dishonest dealings, disillusionment may tempt you to abandon plans. Rows, quarrels, disputes, turmoil, disorder, plans going wrong, partings, unexpected ill fortune. Financial or business problems are only temporary and will be resolved in time. Have patience, reschedule things and persevere.

Six

Improvements, wage increases, rewards. Formal justice or authorities may be helpful. Difficult relationships will improve. Calm after period of turbulence or self-doubt. Steady progress in the area of life of most concern to the questioner. Slow progress but setbacks will be overcome with hard work and persistence and plans will come to fruition.

Seven

Sorrow, warnings, losses, possible death or other loss of a friend. Justice is on your side, intuition may be more helpful than logic and expert opinion. Don't avoid conflict, maximise any advantages. Quarrels with partners, end of romance, relationship break ups, accidents, misunderstandings. Unexpected burden or onerous task. Anxiety over minor issues could cause tension and unnecessary conflicts. Keep a sense of proportion.

Eight

Trouble and disappointment, opposition from others, cancelled plans, obstacles. New contacts and avenues will be fruitful. Change can be achieved with optimism and leaving the past behind. Talking through worries and fears will reveal unconsidered possibilities. Journeys with happy endings, communications that bring good fortune, unexpected arrivals and departures, surprising things about to occur. Resist harsh words or hasty actions, guard health, close relationship could be under strain, business and travel plans could go awry, friends could let you down.

Nine

Bad luck in all things, domestic worries, possible total loss of money, calamities, deaths, natural disasters, destruction, war. You know more than you realise, fears of failure or rejection are unfounded, courage and determination to succeed will overcome obstacles. Family disputes with no long term ill effects. Energy may be at a low ebb due to anxiety. Try not to take on extra burdens.

Take stock of assets and make realistic plans and goals for the future.

Ten

Disappointment card. Misfortune, worry, imprisonment. Will cast a cloud over nearby cards. Better times ahead. May be a necessary natural ending to something so that new beginnings can occur. Stay optimistic and ride things out. Will strengthen surrounding negative cards or reduce the benefits of nearby positive cards. Unwelcome news or worry of a loved one may complicate a situation. Difficult to feel motivated but hang with it as the future will be brighter.

Jack

Dark haired youth, lazy, well-meaning who never quite gets it together. Thoughtlessly or maliciously hurts people, clever, humorous, which can lead to sarcasm and witty criticism. May have reasons for their distrust of life or people. bright, interesting and exciting ideas which are also impractical. Has good intentions but may cause problems. Friendly, witty, good company, immature, irresponsible, unreliable.

Queen

Dark haired woman or feminine person, possibly a widow, unscrupulous, seductive. Gossiping neighbour, disapproving parent-in-law, office harridan - mature woman or feminine person who remains disappointed and critical of people. Can be possessive from fear of being left alone. Surprising loyal and forceful in defending their own. Known for their charm, liveliness and sociability. Independent, capable, efficient, possibly widow or divorcee, ruthlessly ambitious. Strong ally but formidable foe. May be too forthright to have close friends.

King

Dark haired man or masculine person, ambitious, friend of the great but must be careful they don't lose all they have. Disapproving authority figure, harsh judge, over critical parent, pedant whose own knowledge makes them impatient of other's mistakes, perfectionist, may fear their own vulnerability and prefer isolation. Self-confident, popular within their circle, prepared to take a certain amount of risks. Successful or person of standing, a professional in position to help the questioner. Influential and authoritative, demands respect, advice is to be trusted.

Advanced Spreads

32 Card Readings

How to get 32 cards: take out the number cards 2 – 6 – this leaves you with 7-10 in the number cards, the ace and the court cards.

As with the 52 card spreads, you can add shading to your reading by observing the patterns found in the cards dealt. You will find that the general meanings of the suits remain the same as with the 52 card spreads - they are included again in the **Interpretations Keywords** section as a reminder. In addition, you will see that the 32 card spreads include some further pattern combinations that fine tune your reading.

Layouts for 32 Card Readings

The Pyramid

Good for: a simple reading that uses past influences to understand present circumstance and possible future outcomes.

How to do it: This spread used 10 cards – deal them out in a pyramid shape as below, with 4 cards at the base, then 3 in the row above, then 2 in the row above that and 1 at the top.

Read the cards from bottom row to top row. The bottom row is the past influences, each row above advances you in time with the 2nd row up showing present/immediate future, the 3rd row up showing a little further ahead until you land at the top card and the final outcome.

The Temple of Fortune

Good for: a complete reading of the querent's past, present and future.

How to do it: This spread uses all 32 cards, so shuffle thoroughly then deal them out in the pattern below.

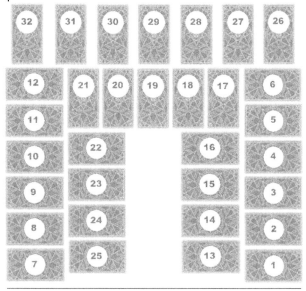

Once you've checked for any patterns and dominant suits, read the cards as follows:

First, read the outside right run of cards from **1 to 6** – these signify the past and concern the major events and outer worldly life.

Next read the inside right run of cards **13 – 16**, which also signify the past but modify the outer past cards. These cards are also concerned with the querents inner mental and spiritual life.

Cards **17 to 21,** the inside horizontal row, represent the present and the concern the major events and outer worldly life.

These are modified by cards **26 – 32,** the top horizontal row, which represent the querent's present inner mental and spiritual life.

Finally, the future cards: **7 – 12,** on the outside left, represent the future major events and outer worldly life with cards **22 – 25,** on the inside left, modifying them, and providing insight in the querent's future inner mental and spiritual life.

Grand Star

Good for: if you're feeling brave! This is a slightly complicated way to read cards and gives a detailed general reading.

How to do it: First pick one of the court cards to represent the querent. This should be placed at the centre of the layout. This card is called the **client card** and is used to focus on the person the reading is done for, as well as provide the centre point for linking situation context for the other cards.

Next deal 21 cards and arrange them as below.

In general, the cards placed above the client card indicate success and future achievements.

The cards below the client card indicate the past and things already achieved.

The cards to the left of the client card indicate obstacles and oppositions.

The cards to the right of the client card indicate the future and any help or assistance to come.

Once you've studied the general patterns of suit and numbers to get a feel for the reading, then it's time for the complicated bit! Cards in the Grand Star are interpreted as pairs, with each card in the pair linked to each other eg. a past situation connected or leading to a future situation. The pairs are read circling the client card, from outside to in, like so:

First pair is cards **13 + 15** – things in the future – success and achievements (card 15) and help and assistance that will contribute to them (card 13).

Next pair is **20 + 18** – in the obstacles and oppositions area – problems overcome in the past (card 18) and things to overcome for future success and achievements (card 20).

Next pair is **14 + 16** – things in the past – the obstacles and oppositions that occurred (card 14) and the help and assistance that occurred or is currently occurring (card 16).

Next pair is **19 + 17** – looking to the future - help and assistance in the past (card 19) that will lead to future success or achievements (card 17).

Next pair is **9 + 5** – still looking to the future – future help and assistance with current issues (card 5) leading to future success or achievements (card 9).

Next pair is **11 + 8** – things in the past (card 8) influencing the future and any help or assistance coming (card 11).

Next pair is **10 + 6** – things in the past or past achievements (card 10) and the obstacles or oppositions experienced (card 6).

Next pair is **12 + 7** – obstacles and oppositions that need overcoming (card 12) before achieving future success (card 7).

Next pair is **3 + 1** – obstacles and oppositions experienced (card 3) linking to past actions or the accomplishing of past achievements (card 1).

Next pair is **4 + 2** – future help and assistance (card 4) needed for future success and achievements (card 2).

Finally, the last card is **card 21** – the final outcome.

Interpretation Keywords for 32 Card Readings

Reversed Cards

While the 52 card readings do not include reversed card interpretations, if you choose to, 32 card readings can. Reversed cards are simply cards that have been dealt with their images upside down.

How to do it: to identify what counts as a reversed card in your deck, you will need to mark one corner or place on the top or bottom of each card. Then, when you shuffle, muddle the cards around the table surface to mix the orientations. You can also choose different ways to flip the cards over when you deal them.

Why use reversed cards? Some readers interpret a reversed card as making the standard meaning more negative or opposite to when it's the right way up; however, some readers prefer to ignore the way up the card was dealt and use the reversed keywords as the possible negative meaning, applying it only if they feel the reading warrants it.

We have included the reversed keywords for all the cards to help you deepen your understanding of the possible interpretations.

Whether you use reversed cards or not is entirely your choice, there is no wrong way to do it so feel free to experiment and find the way that is most comfortable for you.

Suits – general

If one suit is more represented than the others, then the qualities of that suit can modify the individual cards.

Clubs

Ambition, success, career, health, travel, expansion, business partnerships and other business relationships, communication, connections with money, business, and loyalty. Also failure, betrayal and financial worries.

Diamonds

For the life outside the home. Also the suggestion that money and ambitions can only be achieved through hard work. Practical matters, money, property, home, patience, placidity, children, animals.

Hearts

Considered lucky, cover emotions and domestic life, love, affection, friendship, marriage, the family. Also ambitions successfully realised. Intuition, relationships, people in their 20's and 30's.

Spades

Dangers ahead. Misfortunes, loss, suffering, enemies, treachery, failure. Limitations, challenges, tradition, formal learning, justice, assessment and tradition, older people and ageing.

Court cards vs. numbers

If there is a **majority of court cards**, it suggests that personalities are more important to the questioner than situations.

Four cards of the same value can indicate an extreme version of a result, whether joy or sorrow, good fortune or bad.

Three cards of the same value indicate different forces in harmony.

Two cards of the same value suggest that there is either a conflict of interest, a reconciliation or a new connection, depending on the suits involved.

The **Nine of Hearts** will indicate that a wish will be fulfilled in the area suggested by the most dominant suit surrounding it. (Or will lessen the impact of an overly negative reading)

The **Ten of Spades** will indicate disappointment in the area suggested by the most dominant suit surrounding it. (Or will lessen the impact of an overly positive reading)

Other Patterns

When there are groupings of two, three or four cards of the same value immediately next to each other in the spread, these groups should be interpreted first as they are considered to be the most significant and cast an influence on the larger reading.

Two aces – a marriage, a partnership, unusual news. Two red aces = a happy marriage/partnership. A black ace and red ace = unhappy marriage/partnership. One reversed ace = potential marriage/partnership breakdown. Both reversed = more folly and anxiety.

Three aces – temporary anxieties, foolishness, flirtations. The more reversed aces, the more the folly and anxiety increases.

Four aces – separation from money or friends. The more reversed aces, the greater the separation.

Two sevens – new and happy love affair. One seven reversed = deceived in love. Both reversed = regrets in love.

Three sevens – new baby or enterprise. The more reversed sevens, the greater the delay.

Four sevens – mischief makers or enemies, disputes, conspiracies, scandals. The more reversed sevens, the less successful they will be.

Two eights – brief love affair, desire for love. One reversed eight = a flirtation. Both reversed – a misunderstanding.

Three eights – marriage and love. The more reversed eights, the less the commitment.

Four eights – something with mixed failure and success. The more reversed eights, the greater the proportion of failure.

Two nines – small financial gains, reasonable amount of success, important documents to deal with. Each reversed nine lessens the gains/success.

Three nines – happiness, wealth, health. The more reversed nines, the longer the delay.

Four nines – pleasant surprise, good luck. The more reversed nines, the sooner it will happen.

Two tens – good fortune stemming from changes at work or a repaid debt. Each reversed ten delays things.

Three tens – legal and financial problems. Each reversed ten lessens the problems.

Four tens – unexpected good fortune or positive change in circumstances. Each reversed ten lessens the good fortune.

Two jacks – theft or loss, someone with bad intentions towards querent. Each reversed jack brings it closer.

Three jacks – family disagreements. Each reversed jack increases the disagreement.

Four jacks – quarrels, noisy parties. Each reversed jack increased the violence of the quarrel.

Two queens – friendship, minor gossip, interesting meeting with female or feminine friend. One reversed queen = rivalry. Both reversed = betrayal.

Three queens – conversation and visitors, invitations, back biting. The more reversed queens, the greater the gossip and scandal attached to the visit.

Four queens – social gathering or party, scandal. The more reversed queens, the less successful the gathering will be.

Two kings – business partnership or success. One reversed king = partially successful partnership. Both reversed = partnership will fail.

Three kings – new venture, important and beneficial business meetings, success. The more reversed kings, the less successful it will be.

Four kings – good fortune, inheritance, advancement, great success. The more reversed kings, the less it will be.

Suits – individual cards

Clubs

Associated with the element of fire, the tarot suit of wands.

Ace

Good luck, good news, financial papers or letters.

Reversed - Short lived happiness, unpleasant letters.

Seven

Minor money matters.

Reversed – financial problems.

Eight

A dark haired person bringing good fortune or joy.

Reversed – divorce, a legal dispute, unhappy love affair.

Nine

Unexpected money.

Reversed – slight problem, small gift.

Ten

Luxury, prosperity, luck.

Reversed – a journey, business troubles.

Jack

Dark haired youth who's amusing.

Reversed – an insincere lover.

Queen

Dark haired woman or feminine person who's helpful and affectionate.

Reversed – unreliable woman or feminine person.

King

Dark haired man or masculine person who's friendly and honest.

Reversed – minor troubles and worries.

Diamonds

Associated with the element of earth and the tarot suit pentacles.

Ace

Engagement or wedding ring, letter with good news, money.

Reversed – bad news.

Seven

Small gift, criticism, teasing.

Reversed – gossip, minor scandal.

Eight

Short journey, love affair.

Reversed – affections ignored, a separation.

Nine

Anxieties, surprises, news.

Reversed – lovers' quarrels, domestic disputes.

Ten

A major change, a journey, moving house.

Reversed – changes for the worse.

Jack

Person in uniform, employee, a messenger.

Reversed – a trouble maker.

Queen

Fair haired woman or feminine person who's spiteful or talkative.

Reversed – malice.

King

Powerful fair or grey haired man or masculine person.

Reversed – deception, treachery.

Hearts

Associated with the element of water and the tarot suit of cups.

Ace

Domestic happiness, love, good news.

Reversed – short lived happiness, changes, a move.

Seven

Contentment.

Reversed – boredom.

Eight

A wedding, a journey, an invitation.

Reversed – unrequited lover.

Nine

Known as the 'Wish' card – dreams will come true.

Reversed – temporary troubles.

Ten

Happiness, good fortune.

Reversed – a birth, a surprise.

Jack

A fair haired youth or emotionally vulnerable older person, a friend or lover.

Reversed – untrustworthy friend or lover.

Queen

A fair haired woman or feminine person who's dependable and affectionate.

Reversed – woman or feminine person unhappy in love, divorcee or widow.

King

Fair haired man or masculine person who's generous and affectionate.

Reversed – deceitful person.

Spades

Associated with the element of air and the tarot suit of swords.

Ace

Business propositions, emotional satisfaction.

Reversed – death, disappointments, bad news.

Seven

Change of plan, new resolutions.

Reversed – faulty planning, bad advice.

Eight

Impending disappointment, bad news.

Reversed – divorce, quarrels, separation, sorrow.

Nine

Misfortune, loss, failure.

Reversed – unhappiness for a close friend.

Ten

Disappointment card. Grief, confinement, a long journey.

Reversed – minor illness.

Jack

Dark haired youth who's ill-mannered and possibly connected with law or medicine.

Reversed – a traitor.

Queen

Older dark haired woman or feminine person, possibly a widow or divorcee.

Reversed – treacherous and cunning woman or feminine person.

King

Dark haired man or masculine person who's untrustworthy. Lawyer.

Reversed – an enemy.

End Notes

We hope that you have found this guide a useful start to your adventures in cartomancy. If you would like to explore more kinds of divination, take a look at our other books:

Let's Try Tarot

Let's Try Dowsing

The Easy Guide to Self-Employment for Tarot Professionals

Coming Soon:

Let's Try Dice Divination

Let's Try Numerology

Let's Try Runes

And don't forget to check out our website at www.tarot4you.co.uk for our Intuitive Tarot Course and news of forthcoming books, other divinatory related products and what events you can find us at.

Bibliography

Celestine – Fortune Telling (Siena, 1998)

Eason, Cassandra – A Complete Guide to Divination (Piatkus, 1998) [1]

Fenton, Sasha - The Fortune-Teller's Workbook (The Aquarian Press, 1988)

King, Francis A. – The Complete Fortune-Teller (Guild Publishing, 1989)

Unknown – Predicting (Harper Collins Publishers, 1991)

About the Author

Ann J. Clark is an editor and author in multiple genres of fiction and non-fiction; with a passion for SF geekery, history, mythology and visiting ancient sites. She discovered the tarot and associated divination practices as a teenager and has read tarot online and in one-to-one environments.

You can visit her website at
www.jennybarber.co.uk

Ann J. Clark

Printed in Great Britain
by Amazon